M109A6 PALADINS

BY DENNY VON FINN

EPIC

BELLWETHER MEDIA · MINNEAPOLIS, MN

EPIC BOOKS are no ordinary books. They burst with intense action, high-speed heroics, and shadows of the unknown. Are you ready for an Epic adventure?

This edition first published in 2013 by Bellwether Media, Inc.

No part of this publication may be reproduced in whole or in part without written permission of the publisher. For information regarding permission, write to Bellwether Media, Inc., Attention: Permissions Department, 5357 Penn Avenue South, Minneapolis, MN 55419.

Library of Congress Cataloging-in-Publication Data

Von Finn, Denny.
 M109A6 Paladins / by Denny Von Finn.
    p. cm. – (Epic books: military vehicles)
 Includes bibliographical references and index.
 Summary: "Engaging images accompany information about M109A6 Paladins. The combination of high-interest subject matter and light text is intended for students in grades 2 through 7"–Provided by publisher.
 Audience: Grades 2-7.
 ISBN 978-1-60014-820-0 (hbk. : alk. paper)
 1. M109 Paladin (Howitzer)–Juvenile literature. I. Title.
 UF652.V66 2013
 623.4'2-dc23   2012007676

Printed in the United States of America, North Mankato, MN.

TABLE OF CONTENTS

M109A6 PALADINS

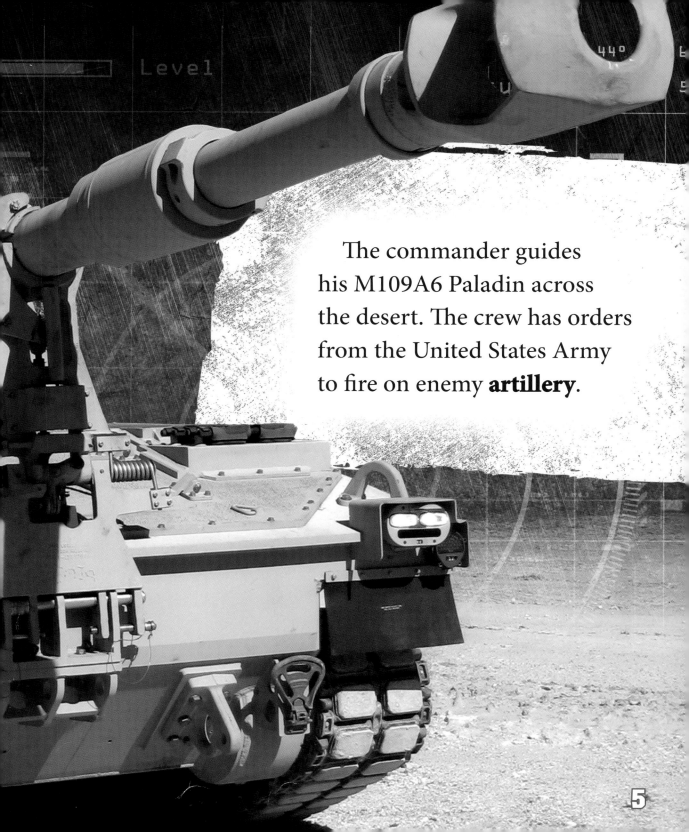

The commander guides his M109A6 Paladin across the desert. The crew has orders from the United States Army to fire on enemy **artillery**.

The Paladin stops and fires a **round** from its **cannon**. Smoke rises in the distance. An enemy gun has been destroyed!

Paladin Fact

A Paladin round weighs up to 100 pounds (45 kilograms). It can hit targets more than 18 miles (30 kilometers) away.

143

The Paladin moves to another position. It will be hard for the enemy to find this **self-propelled** artillery.

WEAPONS AND FEATURES

TURRET

TRACKS

A Paladin looks like a tank. It has thick **armor** and **tracks**. A cannon is attached to its **turret**.

CANNON

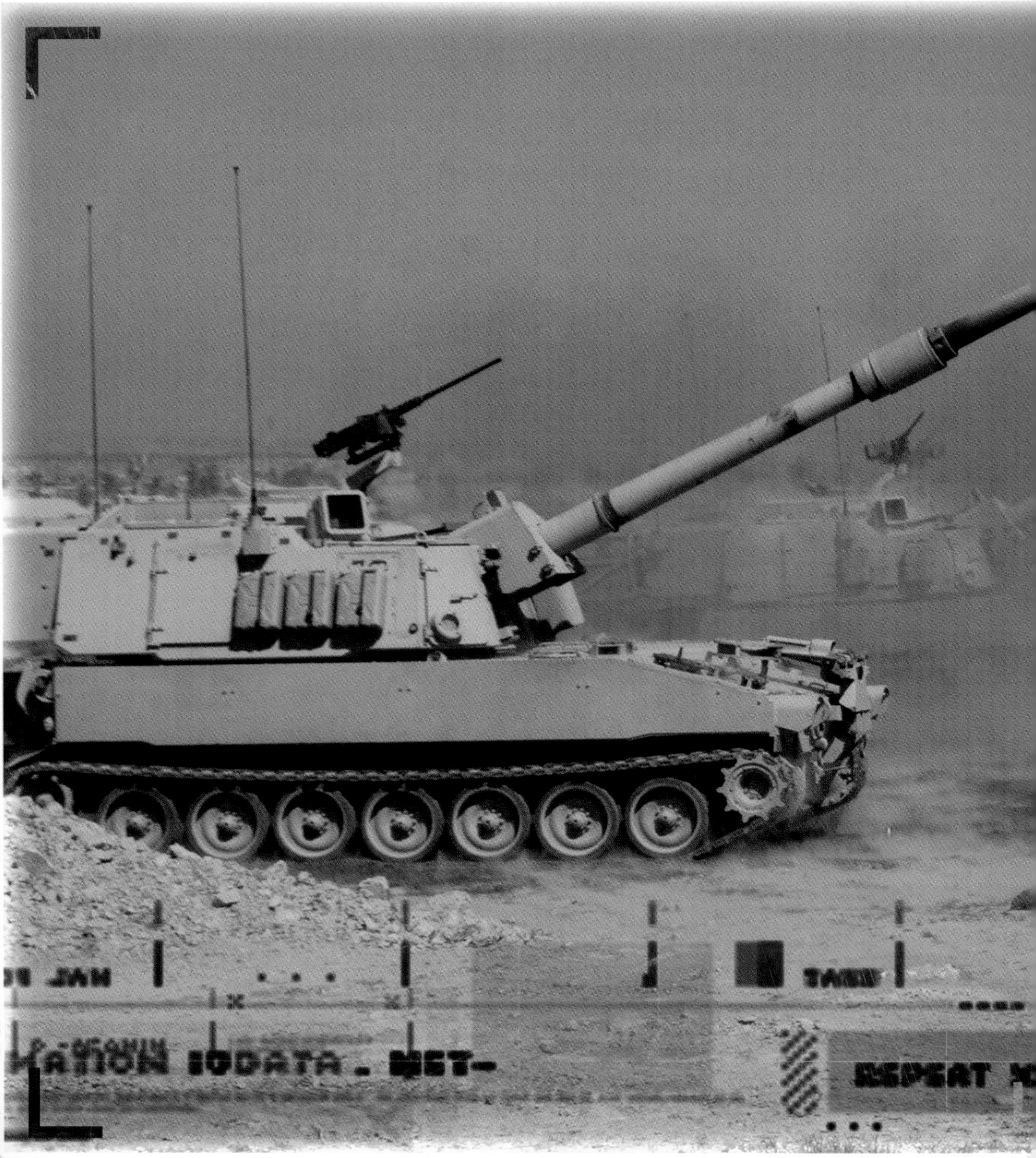

Paladin Fact

A computer helps a Paladin crew aim the cannon.

However, a Paladin is different from a tank. A tank fires rounds straight at a target. A Paladin shoots rounds upward. The rounds fall on targets from above.

A Paladin has a crew of four. The gunner and loader fire the cannon. The driver steers the Paladin. The commander oversees the **mission**.

COMMANDER

LOADER

M109A6 PALADIN MISSIONS

The Paladin's mission is to protect **infantry**. Paladins can travel with infantry or stay behind them to give support.

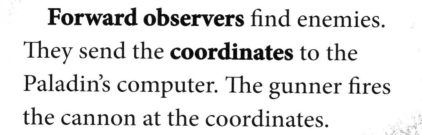

Forward observers find enemies. They send the **coordinates** to the Paladin's computer. The gunner fires the cannon at the coordinates.

FORWARD OBSERVER

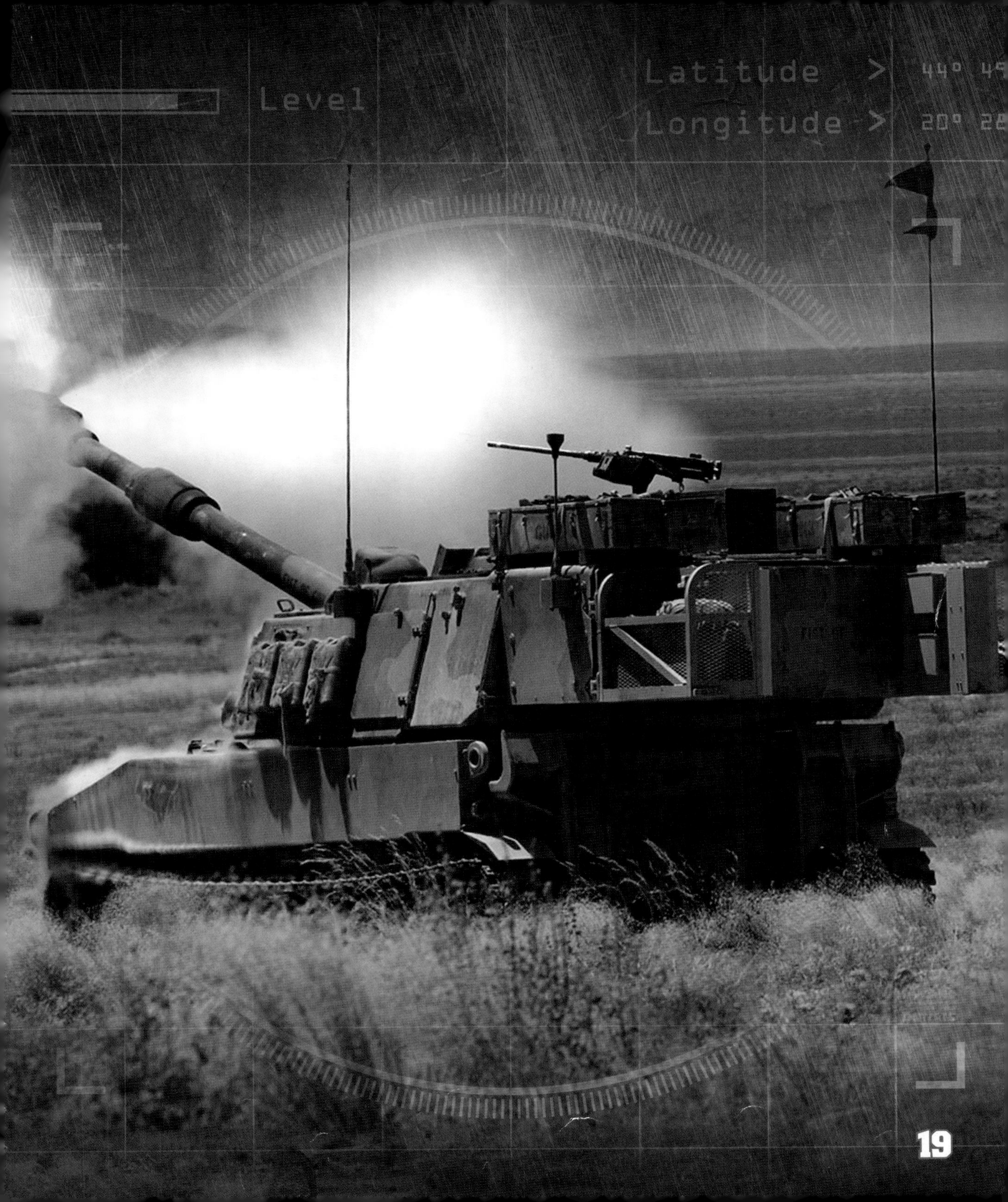
Level
Latitude > 44°
Longitude > 20°

The Paladin performed well in the **War on Terror**. Soldiers on the ground can count on the support of the mighty Paladin!

VEHICLE BREAKDOWN: M109A6 PALADIN

Used By:	U.S. Army
Entered Service:	1991
Length (with Gun):	31.7 feet (9.7 meters)
Height:	11.9 feet (3.6 meters)
Width:	10.3 feet (3.1 meters)
Weight (Fully Loaded):	63,600 pounds (28,850 kilograms)
Top Speed:	40 miles (64.4 kilometers) per hour
Maximum Firing Range:	18.6 miles (30 kilometers)
Maximum Rate of Fire:	4 rounds per minute
Crew:	4
Weapons:	155mm cannon, 12.7mm machine gun
Primary Mission:	artillery support

GLOSSARY

armor—thick plates that cover the Paladin to protect the crew from enemy fire

artillery—large guns and cannons that fire rounds great distances

cannon—the main gun of a Paladin

coordinates—numbers that tell the location of something

forward observers—soldiers who spot enemies and send their locations to artillery crews

infantry—soldiers who travel on the ground

mission—a military task

round—a single shot; each round has all of the parts needed to fire one shot.

self-propelled—able to move on its own

tracks—long belts that wrap around the wheels of a Paladin; tracks help a Paladin grip the ground.

turret—the part of a Paladin that rotates and holds the cannon

War on Terror—a conflict that began in 2001; the War on Terror has been fought in Afghanistan, Pakistan, and Iraq

TO LEARN MORE

At the Library

Alvarez, Carlos. *M109A6 Paladins*. Minneapolis, Minn.: Bellwether Media, 2010.

Baker, David. *M109 Paladin*. Vero Beach, Fla.: Rourke Pub., 2007.

Graham, Ian. *Military Vehicles*. Chicago, Ill.: Heinemann Library, 2008.

On the Web

Learning more about M109A6 Paladins is as easy as 1, 2, 3.

1. Go to www.factsurfer.com.

2. Enter "M109A6 Paladins" into the search box.

3. Click the "Surf" button and you will see a list of related Web sites.

With factsurfer.com, finding more information is just a click away.

INDEX